SH*T

By

Virginia Johnson

(SMH – FML – WTF)

The Good Stuff

Editing

No, obviously.

Formatting and Cover

Anytime Author Promotions

ISBN-13: 978-1977670465

ISBN-10: 1977670466

Dedication

Where to begin? I suppose I will start with the obvious shitheads that started this whole series in the first place. The KV Discord girls. I blame the shit out of you. While you sit back and watch as I am blasted for releasing such a shitty book, I am reminded of the times that I liked you. The like was real and I was genuine about that shit. Now? Now, I was to paste your names all over the cover and hope the rage that is sure to come falls on the innocent shoulders of your laughing asses. For the record – The like is now Love!

My PA, Janneke – I blame you the most. The love is real ;)

this is mostly your fault

Table of Contents

Vietnamese

Mongolian

Telugu

Urdu

Finnish

Croatian

Ukranian

Tamil

Marathi

Xhosa

Welsh

Swedish

Kyrgyz

Scots Gaelic

Pashto

Greek

Yiddish

Serbian

Luxembourgish

Kannada

Turkish

About ME

Seriously?

There it is... SH*T, in short.

For real, though.

This SH*T has ended...

Why SH*T?

Apparently, it is necessary to warn you that I did very little research on this shit. Meaning, if you are offended by anything in this book and want to execute me for the spelling or true meaning of any of the translations, then fuck off. I don't speak any of these languages and I am only here to give you a little insight on the fact that people shit, people are shit, shit is shit, shit happens and shittier things happen to shitty people. I have now given you the opportunity to say it in a different language. Now that we have clarified that I have absolutely no confidence in you enjoying this shitty disaster, please continue.

So, I have been asked on too many occasions, "Why the fuck do you think releasing this shit is a good idea?"

My response to everyone that asks? "I have no idea why this shit is so important." Followed by intense laughter and shitty comments. I completely understand that there is no real reason for any of the books in this series to exist. If there were, they would be written. But, as I can tell, they are not; at least not in this format. If they were, everyone would own it. I know I would've wasted the $.99 on a piece of SH*T.

I swear there was a reason for these books and I have no fucking idea what it is. All that I know is that I am stuck with finishing a dare that I couldn't turn down. Hence, F*CK and SH*T. (more to come). Let me continue with this shitty "Why," before everyone gets their panties in a bunch.

There is a point in life that makes every human sit back and reminisce on their shitty existence and reflect. The shit that has happened to them or the amount of shit that has been dropped on their doorstep has started to pile up. When the shit doesn't remove itself, you are left with nothing more than a security system that smells like the death of a shit demon, lit on fire, abandoned at a shit plant, wrapped in saran wrap, left outside in the Florida summer heat for days AND dropped on your porch for the unwanted visitors to march their shitty penny loafers in to. Sounds fun, right?

Hell no, that doesn't sound fun. It sounds like one hell of a shitty mess! No-one in their right mind would want that hanging out on their welcome mat. At least, I wouldn't. You may be a shit collector, but I can guarantee that I most certainly am not.

As I was saying, life can be a shitty thing to live if you allow it to suck. Am I starting to sound like some kind of shit-brewing "Self-Help" advertisement? Yeah, well... it isn't. It is only an attempt to describe shit in its natural form. For fuck sake, I am rambling.

Basically, there are many ways that the word, "SHIT" can be used. Although not commonly used in the professional corporate America world, because swearing is frowned upon, I can guarantee that at some point every single person, including your precious two-year old has said, "Oh, Shit!"

Still in denial? Good, cause if you were, that would be fucking ridiculous. So, now I have given you a way to say "SHIT" in the corporate world, in front of your kids, at church, the kiddie park... wherever. This way you can say something like, "You little shit!" to the toddler that just kicked you in the shin, without offending 'Super Mom' on the next bench.

Gone are the days that you have to watch your mouth around sensitive hypocritical individuals that say it *MORE THAN YOU DO!* Now, you can smile politely to the possibly offended party and whisper, "eat paska" and hope to hell that they don't speak Finnish. Of course, if they do, they will only drop their jaw, widen their eyes and give you ample time to resort back to your native language and clarify your statement, "As I said, eat shit."

Some of you are thinking this through to the end. Maybe I am right? Maybe I am wrong? Maybe, just maybe, I don't really give a shit? That sounds like a more reasonable response to what I think about a book obnoxiously titled, SH*T. I mean, did you really expect much more from me? Oh, you did. Well, that sucks because this book isn't going to get any better. Actually, it is only going to get shittier as we delve in to the 40 different ways to say it.

Please, keep in mind, as I had said with F*CK, I didn't do much research on the actual translations. Honestly, this shit was more thought out and took a little longer only because shit got in the way of me finishing it. But, I did ask, "How do you say shit in Dutch?"

Thankfully, I was told because the one I had found was wrong or Americanized for the tourists that would still use the word "Shit." What I am trying to say with all this shit is that I did do some research and found that the translated word for shit is shit in Dutch, but it was WRONG.

I bet you are now thinking that you need to get to the translation just to see what it is. Don't worry, I would look up that shit first, too!

So, without any further ado... I give you a book full of, literally, shit!

English

Shit

SKILL PRACTICE

Virginia Johnson

Gujarati

છી

SKILL PRACTICE

Haitian Creole

Kaka

SKILL PRACTICE

Virginia Johnson

Arabic

القرف

SKILL PRACTICE

Chinese

拉屎

SKILL PRACTICE

French

Merde

SKILL PRACTICE

_____

_____

_____

_____

_____

_____

_____

_____

_____

_____

Norwegian

Dritt

SKILL PRACTICE

_____

_____

_____

_____

_____

_____

_____

_____

_____

_____

_____

_____

_____

Portuguese

Merda

SKILL PRACTICE

Latin

Stercore

SKILL PRACTICE

Virginia Johnson

Russian

Дерьмо

SKILL PRACTICE

_____

_____

_____

_____

_____

_____

_____

_____

_____

_____

Japanese

たわごと

SKILL PRACTICE

Virginia Johnson

Spanish

Mierda

SKILL PRACTICE

_____

_____

_____

_____

_____

_____

_____

_____

_____

German

Scheisse

SKILL PRACTICE

_____

_____

_____

_____

_____

_____

_____

_____

_____

_____

_____

_____

_____

_____

Virginia Johnson

Lithuanian

Šūdas

SKILL PRACTICE

_____

_____

_____

_____

_____

_____

_____

_____

_____

_____

Hindi

मल

SKILL PRACTICE

Thai

อื

SKILL PRACTICE

Azerbaijani

Pox

SKILL PRACTICE

Slovak

Hovno

SKILL PRACTICE

Filipino

Tae

SKILL PRACTICE

_____

_____

_____

_____

_____

_____

_____

_____

_____

_____

_____

_____

Dutch

Poep

SKILL PRACTICE

Vietnamese

Dơ bẩn

SKILL PRACTICE

Virginia Johnson

Mongolian

өмхий баас

SKILL PRACTICE

_____

_____

_____

_____

_____

_____

_____

_____

_____

_____

Telugu

ఒంటి

SKILL PRACTICE

_____

_____

_____

_____

_____

_____

_____

_____

_____

_____

_____

_____

_____

_____

_____

Virginia Johnson

Urdu

شٹ

SKILL PRACTICE

Finnish

Paska

SKILL PRACTICE

Croatian

Paska

SKILL PRACTICE

Ukranian

Лайно

SKILL PRACTICE

Tamil

மலம்

SKILL PRACTICE

Marathi

कचरा

SKILL PRACTICE

Xhosa

Ikaka

SKILL PRACTICE

Welsh

Cachu

SKILL PRACTICE

Swedish

Skit

SKILL PRACTICE

Kyrgyz

Какая

SKILL PRACTICE

Scots Gaelic

Fhalbh

SKILL PRACTICE

_____

_____

_____

_____

_____

_____

_____

_____

_____

_____

_____

_____

Pashto

چنتلي

SKILL PRACTICE

Greek

Σκατά

SKILL PRACTICE

___

Yiddish

דרעק

SKILL PRACTICE

_____

_____

_____

_____

_____

_____

_____

_____

_____

_____

_____

_____

Serbian

Говно

SKILL PRACTICE

_____

_____

_____

_____

_____

_____

_____

_____

_____

Luxembourgish

SchŠiss

SKILL PRACTICE

Virginia Johnson

Kannada

ತೌಟ

SKILL PRACTICE

_____

_____

_____

_____

_____

_____

_____

_____

_____

_____

Turkish

Bok

SKILL PRACTICE

About ME

Follow Virginia Johnson and stay up to date!

Facebook: https://facebook.com/AuthorVirginiaJohnson/

Website: https://authorvirginiajohnson.com/

Twitter: https://twitter.com/AuthorVJohnson

Instagram: https://www.instagram.com/charmedchic24/

Amazon: http://www.amazon.com/Virginia-L-Johnson/e/B01E88KI5Q/ref=ntt_dp_epwbk_0

Newsletter: http://tinyletter.com/VirginiaLeeJohnson

Fan Group: https://www.facebook.com/groups/KylesHarem/

SH*T

Seriously?

Hanging in there for just one more shitty surprise?
Fine then....
Join our fan group
"Shit" is the second least offensive thing in there.

Fan Group: https://www.facebook.com/groups/KylesHarem/

SH*T

There it is... SH*T, in short.

I guess it is a little more than short. I mean, obviously, there is no shortage of shit. You may actually be feeling an increased abundance of shit if you take in to consideration the ridiculous amount of translations that I found for it. Your tongue may feel like shit if you tried to sound out each and every one of them. Ya did, didn't ya? I know you fucking did, don't lie. You may have even tried to sound out the ones that aren't even in your normal alphabet. Admit it! Don't worry about what anyone else thinks, they all did it too. Except me. I didn't and I will silently judge the shit out of you for doing it. But don't feel ashamed, everyone else is being equally judged.

I do hope you enjoyed this piece of shit book. If not, well, there isn't really a complaints department. So, grab your phone, take it to the shitter (everyone does it), leave a shit or two while browsing your fav social media site, and you'll either forget all about this book, or be constantly reminded EACH AND EVERY time you see a toilet.

You're Welcome.

SH*T

For real, though.

Are we really going to have this conversation again? This is where you should be pulling yourself back together. You don't want to look like a complete fool to your family, as they have already watched you mumble incoherently to yourself as you stared at your phone – LIKE A CRAZY PERSON.

They will only laugh at you for a few seconds if you do the following –

1) Power down the phone or e-reader – whatever drug of choice you have.

2) Turn to your family. This is very important.

3) Ask yourself this question – Do you have a problem with this book?

If you answered "YES" – Continue – If you answered "NO" Skip to #5

4) "Yes" People – Put your hands on your hips and in your meanest, most ferocious growly voice yell, "I have a problem with SHIT!"

Still No Judging

5) "NO" peeps – Look to each and every member of your family with a smile on your face and say, "You all have to read this SH*T!"

Do you regret sticking around, yet? No? Good, you'll love the next installment...

SH*T

This SH*T has ended...

Wipe and fold. Wipe and fold.

Now, stop! Seriously, STOP!

If you wipe more than 2 times you stimulate your anus. Basically, you are masturbating immediately following a shit.

Just, No.

SKILL PRACTICE

SKILL PRACTICE

SKILL PRACTICE

SKILL PRACTICE

SKILL PRACTICE

SKILL PRACTICE

SKILL PRACTICE

SKILL PRACTICE

SKILL PRACTICE

_____

_____

_____

_____

_____

_____

_____

_____

_____

_____

_____

_____

_____

_____

_____

_____

SKILL PRACTICE

SKILL PRACTICE

SKILL PRACTICE

SKILL PRACTICE

SKILL PRACTICE

_____

_____

_____

_____

_____

_____

_____

_____

_____

_____

_____

_____

_____

SKILL PRACTICE

SKILL PRACTICE

SH*T

SKILL PRACTICE

SKILL PRACTICE

SKILL PRACTICE

_____

_____

_____

_____

_____

_____

_____

_____

_____

_____

_____

_____

_____

_____

_____

_____

SKILL PRACTICE

SKILL PRACTICE

_____

_____

_____

_____

_____

_____

_____

_____

_____

_____

_____

_____

_____

SKILL PRACTICE

SKILL PRACTICE

SKILL PRACTICE

SKILL PRACTICE

_____

_____

_____

_____

_____

_____

_____

_____

_____

_____

_____

_____

_____

_____

SKILL PRACTICE

SKILL PRACTICE

_____

_____

_____

_____

_____

_____

_____

_____

_____

_____

_____

_____

_____

SKILL PRACTICE

SKILL PRACTICE

SKILL PRACTICE

_____

_____

_____

_____

_____

_____

_____

_____

_____

_____

_____

_____

_____

SKILL PRACTICE

SKILL PRACTICE

SKILL PRACTICE

SKILL PRACTICE

SKILL PRACTICE

SKILL PRACTICE

SKILL PRACTICE

SKILL PRACTICE

SKILL PRACTICE

SKILL PRACTICE

SKILL PRACTICE

SKILL PRACTICE

SKILL PRACTICE

SKILL PRACTICE

SKILL PRACTICE

SKILL PRACTICE

SKILL PRACTICE

_____

_____

_____

_____

_____

_____

_____

_____

_____

_____

_____

_____

_____

_____

_____

SKILL PRACTICE

SKILL PRACTICE

SKILL PRACTICE

SKILL PRACTICE

SKILL PRACTICE

SKILL PRACTICE

SKILL PRACTICE

SKILL PRACTICE

SKILL PRACTICE

SKILL PRACTICE

SKILL PRACTICE

SKILL PRACTICE

SKILL PRACTICE

SKILL PRACTICE

SKILL PRACTICE

SKILL PRACTICE

SKILL PRACTICE

SKILL PRACTICE

_____

_____

_____

_____

_____

_____

_____

_____

_____

_____

_____

_____

_____

SKILL PRACTICE

SKILL PRACTICE

SKILL PRACTICE

SKILL PRACTICE

SKILL PRACTICE

SKILL PRACTICE

SKILL PRACTICE

SKILL PRACTICE

SKILL PRACTICE

SKILL PRACTICE

SKILL PRACTICE

Made in the USA
Lexington, KY
18 May 2018